The Princess Bride
and The Predator

Murder or Manslaughter

by

Gloria De Laurentis Ferrara

with Joseph Verola

1

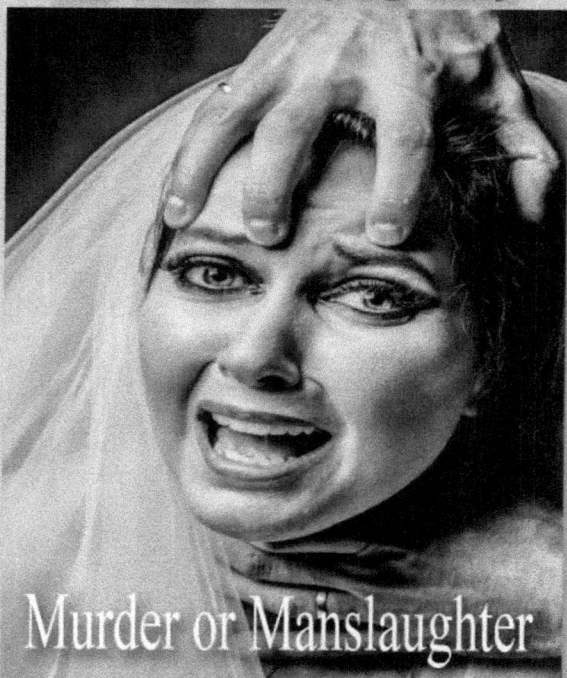

The Princess Bride
and The Predator
My True Terrifying Story

Murder or Manslaughter

Gloria De Laurentis
with Joseph Verola

Co-Author Dedication

I want to thank Gloria for all her truthfulness and courage to tell this horrific true story of mental and physical abuse. I could not have detailed what horrific acts that caused Gloria to shoot and kill her husband Patrick, without the input from her loving sisters: Theresa, Tracy, and Ashley.

Special acknowledgement must be attributed to Gloria's attorney, Lisa Schreibersdorf. Without her support and hard legal work, Gloria and many other women, who suffer from mental and physical abuse who fought back, would find themselves in prisons or mental intuitions. Lisa Schreibersdorf, is now the Executive Director at Brooklyn Defender Services and continues to fight for the rights of battered and abused women.

Joe V

Preface

As I prepared to meet Gloria and learned
more about her story, I had no idea what Gloria
would look like, or act like. Would she be mean,
nasty, or sweet? From what I'd was told, when she
married Patrick at fifteen, she was drop dead
gorgeous.

Finally, I was intrigued listening to Gloria's
story, firsthand; never sat down and listened to
someone that murdered a spouse. And yet, I invited
this woman into my home.

Murder or manslaughter? I listened and
wrote her story; fighting hard not to judge. I took
notes and asked questions while she graphically
reminisced the relentless shooting of her husband
after years of abuse and being a battered woman.
I've met many women that were in similar situations

and I have no respect for men who feel a need to control women and beat them into submission.

It was June, 2013, when Gloria, now forty-seven, walked into my living room. Time and circumstances hadn't been kind to her, although, I could still see a beautiful, yet tortured soul, who's innocent beauty was stolen when just a child.

I began writing Gloria's story from her point of view. As I got to know her sisters, Ashley, Theresa and Tracey, I was given deeper insights into what made Gloria pull the trigger, killing a man she once loved unconditionally.

Gloria - Welcome to My World

I was born Gloria Petti, in Philadelphia, on June 24, 1966 and raised by a loving mother, to whom I should have listened. My mother divorced my father when I was four and I only saw him one more time after that which I regretted.

Shortly after the divorce, my father's brother who always loved my mother, moved in to take his place. I grew up with my two younger sisters, Theresa, born October 4, 1969, and Tracy, born October 31, 1970. We lived in a nice, two-story home with four bedrooms and a back yard with an above ground swimming pool. Theresa and Tracy called our uncle father, but I refused; maybe that's why, at one point, in anger, he threw me down a flight of stairs and broke my nose. My mother refused accept any more abuse in our home and in 1972 she moved us to Brooklyn, New York.

The abuse now moved with us. In 1977, Patrick walked into my life, then on March 12, 1991

I closed my eyes and started shooting, until the gun clicked empty. Now, here is my side of the story, feel free to judge me, murder or manslaughter, guilty or innocent?

Gloria - Enter Patrick De Laurentis

I was eleven when I first met Patrick De Laurentis, age twenty-two, at my Cousin Jeannie's home in Brooklyn. She was a distant cousin, but I thought of her as a loving aunt. My mother, Frances Petti and sister Tracy were there, along with Jeannie's two kids, Faith age five and Troy age three. Patrick was Jeannie's boyfriend. They'd been living together for about a year, but that day would tell myself I will marry him someday. A childhood crush, you'd think.

We were all sitting in Jeannie's living room talking when Patrick entered the house. He was gorgeous, 5'11', about 170 lbs., dark hair as he strolled over to us with a smile. He then immediately started spraying everyone with shaving cream, my mother being first. We were all laughing and having fun as we tried to take control of the can of shaving cream to return the greeting with foam; there was shaving cream everywhere.

8

I always looked older for my age, not dramatically, but at eleven I looked at least fourteen. A couple of years seemed like a lot when you're just a kid. I dressed the part. I had boobs, a nice butt and I think I looked sexy for my age. I really liked all the attention I received from him. I was going to be his Princess and he was going to be my "Knight in Shining Armor." I could tell just by the way he smiled at me and kept checking me out. An imagination can be dangerous.

Later that afternoon, Patrick took me into one of the bedrooms and showed me pictures of naked boys and girls. I wasn't shocked, I was intrigued, and I didn't tell anyone. If I did, I knew I would never be allowed to see him again.

Baby Sitting

The week after the shaving cream episode, Patrick came to my mother's house and asked her if I could spend the night at Cousin Jeannie's to babysit her kids. My mother agreed, I was excited, it was my first babysitting job. I was going to get paid, and didn't care, I was going to see and spend some time with Patrick.

Later that evening, when Jeannie and Patrick returned from the movies, I went into Faith's room and laid down in the bed with her to sleep. At about two-thirty in the morning, Patrick came into the room, woke up Faith, wanting her to go with him into the living room. She seemed scared, started crying, saying she didn't want to go with him. Naive, I sat up and when he looked at me, I told him I would go with him instead. Once in the living room he told me to take off my clothes and I did. He just photographed me. Looking back, I wasn't scared, he made me feel sexy - another obvious mistake. Looking back, if that was my daughter, I would have killed him.

Playtime at Cousin Jeannie's

During the following year, I spent more time with Patrick at my Cousin Jeannie's house. I saw and did things with him that would cause any parent to believe in capital punishment. There was no excuse, I was just too sexually motivated, so desirous of his attention, that I enjoyed my time with him. I learned recently that women can have higher than normal levels of testosterone and it can affect their sex drive. Maybe, that was part of my problem?

Anyway, if you were to ask my sister Tracy and Theresa, they would tell you that I was very sexual as early as eleven; that I would quietly go into their beds and lie on top of either one of them at different times and rub against them, as if having sex, until they woke up and push me off.

I don't know why I was never shocked or frightened when Patrick would let me watch as he had sex with a teenage girl named Sherry or while

Jeannie was having sex with a boy named Tommy. He also allowed me to watch while he was having sex with my cousin.

Patrick was incredibly talented and would sing love songs to me. He was into rock n' roll, played the guitar, had a great voice, and sounded a lot like the BG's. If he would have focused on his music instead of using drugs, and abusing children, he could have had the potential to be a success in the music business. If?

I had my first orgasm when he went down on me at age twelve. Although, we never had intercourse until we were married - a pervert, with morals. It wasn't that he didn't want to, after all he was having sex with my friend, Sherry, who was only thirteen. I believe he knew he could get away with it with her, but he wasn't sure if he could take a chance with me because of my mother. However, I would give him blow jobs. I liked that, but never got used to him coming in my mouth. Let's throw out the morals.

I can remember Patrick torturing Faith and Troy. I saw him put hot pennies in their hands and hold them closed. Sometimes, he covered their heads with a plastic bag until they almost passed out and then hang them by their feet from the third-floor window. Strange, but I never thought that we were being abused. Like Patrick, I came to think it was funny.

Nude Photos
Days of Wine and Roses

During that first year, Patrick took dozens of nude photos of my friend, Ellen and myself. Patrick tried to make it fun. We all drank a little wine, as he tried to be artistic, having us wear makeup, our hair pinned up, lying on a bed of roses. Most of photos where just pornographic, a couple twelve-year-old-girls, spread eagled on a bed with whipped cream on our vaginas.

Patrick didn't know, but I took some of his pictures and hid them in my dresser, underneath some clothes. Maybe I wanted them found, because shortly after, my mother found the nude photos of me and other young girls. She was furious.

My mother was a single parent and an alcoholic. She often left us at home alone while she went to the local bar. I guess she did the best she could. She called the police and had Patrick arrested. He was able to get off with a reprimand and was ordered not to be around me. Unfortunately, sex offenders were treated much differently in those days.

Patrick later told me, "My father paid the judge off, with $20,000.

Sister Tracy's - Take on Cousin Jeannie

I always found it hard to believe that my cousin Jeannie, would be involved with Patrick's child abuse and the sexual activities that Gloria described. I wasn't there, although I do know she broke up with Patrick as soon as she learned that he was spending time with Gloria, and learned of the nude photos of Gloria and her daughter.

As for Patrick, he was a sleazy pervert. There was this one time, he was driving me home, when I was only eight or nine. Along the way he pulled into a cemetery, stopped and shut the engine. He looked at me, starting to open his pants and asked me if I had ever seen a man's cock. I jumped into the back seat and he followed me and began jerking off. I jumped back in the front seat and he wanted to cum on my face. I fought and scratched his face and he stopped. He threatened me, saying that if I told anyone, they would believe him not a dumb kid.

Joe on Tracey

I liked Tracey. She was honest about herself. Most commendable, was the great job she was doing raising her teenage daughter, a very straight A student. She sang in the local church, liked boys, but not as priority and most importantly, was street smart about sexual predators. Sadly, Tracy was also subjected to mental and physical abuse from the father of her teenage daughter.

The Letter

Two years after the nude photo incident, when I was fourteen, Patrick wrote my mother a letter. In it, he apologized and part of what he wrote said, "I know what I did was wrong, and I would like to and need to tell Gloria the same." My mother agreed, with the understanding that I would only be allowed to see him once.

After seeing him, I knew I could not live without him anymore and I started running away to be with him. My mother objected and we fought constantly. She would find me and bring me home. I tried to kill myself by overdosing on Valium. After that, she reluctantly allowed me to see him.

Patrick said he loved me. He played the guitar and sang love songs to me. He told me, "You're going to be my Princess and I'm going to be your Prince."

What a princess? What a prince? What a fool I was. He would feed me with drugs, pot,

19

cocaine, acid and other pills. He was a sick fuck, but I still thought I loved the asshole.

Tracey on Mom

My mother tried to stop Gloria from seeing Patrick. Gloria was like a bulldog. She argued with my mother constantly and would physically beat her up when she tried to stop her from seeing him. My mom finally, reluctantly gave up.

1981 Married to the Devil

In 1981 I was an immature fifteen and Patrick twenty-six, when my mother realized she couldn't stop me from seeing him, and so she allowed me to marry Patrick and become his princess.

On the day we were married, I became Mrs. Patrick De Laurentis, and related to Dino De Laurentiis. Patrick was second cousin to the famous movie director, who changed his name to De Laurentiis, with two ii, when he became well known.

I wore a beautiful white satin dress as we were married in a lovely chapel in South Carolina. Returning home to a large reception at my in-laws' home, our family and friends filled the house and backyard. Everyone was having a good time as I sat there with my white satin money purse, receiving envelopes filled with cash. It was like they were throwing it at us—so many Italians, so much money. We were so much in love.

Once married, we rented an apartment in Brooklyn and made it our home. That is when, to my surprise, I learned Patrick was a drug dealer.

I felt his friend Sonny was jealous, because he really liked me and let me know it. Sonny, Patrick's father, and his brother were cops. I think that's where Patrick got all the drugs he sold, like crack, cocaine, heroin, and pills. We cut up slabs of crack and sold it out of the apartment. He wouldn't let me work because he was very jealous. He liked me when I was eleven, at fifteen he couldn't keep his hands off me.

In the beginning of our marriage, Patrick was great. He was concerned about me and my health. He would not let me drink, although he allowed me to smoke pot. I didn't know why, until I smoked some weed and my cousin gave me a vodka and orange juice to drink. I got so drunk and sick, I walked down to the peer, fell and wound up busting my knee open. Patrick carried me home and told off my cousin. He was my protector?

The Stork Was On His Way

It didn't take long before the honeymoon was over, and all hell broke loose. Shortly after we moved into our apartment, I became pregnant with our first son, Patrick Jr..

I've been told not all husbands react well when they find their wife is pregnant. When I told Patrick, he smiled at me, then attempted to drown me in the bathtub. He stopped and he let me live (that was his first big mistake). I don't know why, he didn't talk much, but I was thankful. I do know he didn't want me messing up my body by being pregnant, he resented the extra weight, and stretch marks. That's when the physical abuse started, as I saw it.

On August 6, 1982 Patrick Jr. was born, 10 lbs. 15 ounces. Throughout my pregnancy, I didn't do drugs, even though Patrick pushed them on me. Sometimes, I would fake taking them, just to stop him from hitting me. I wanted my baby to be healthy. I wanted to do something right.

Because he was dealing drugs, Patrick became paranoid and insisted that I carry a gun with me at all times. So, I did (that was his second big mistake).

That is also when I began to believe Patrick's family may have been connected to the mob.

I was so proud of my baby boy. I would take him for a stroll, my gun tucked under the carriage mattress.

After the birth of Patrick Jr. the level of abuse kicked up a notch. I was no longer his princess and he was no longer my Knight in Shining Armor. That is when he started me on drugs. He put a strap around my arm, put the needle in, took it out with some blood, mixed it with crack and stuck it back up my vein. My head just exploded. I felt so good I was hooked. The next day, as soon as he left the apartment, I tried doing it myself. I had four needle marks in my arm without getting high. The next step down on the ladder of addiction was when he introduced me to heroin. Thankfully, I didn't like it. I preferred Crack, as my drug of choice.

Once I was hooked, he brought men into our home to have sex with me. I couldn't understand why a man who said he loved me would want me to have sex with other men. He said I needed experience and if I refused, he'd let them rape me. He liked watching me having sex with other men. I knew he was charging them to fuck me, but I wasn't seeing any of the money. No wonder I'm so fucked up (that was his third big mistake). Mine was not finding a way to leave.

Patrick also used drugs, and when he did, it made him meaner. It didn't take much to provoke him. If I bought the wrong juice, I would get a beating. If I didn't answer fast enough, I suffered the consequences. He would put a pillow over my face and punch me in the head. One time, I came back to the car with Hi C instead of Juicy Juice and he literally kicked me out of the car with his father watching. I didn't deserve that and his father told him not to ever do it again, but he did.

Patrick now—instead of calling me his Princess named me Satan's daughter. He didn't care what he said or did to me. He would embarrass and humiliate me in front of friends and family. On our bedroom wall he painted 666, representing the day I was born; the first 6, for the month of June, the second 6 for the 24th day 2+4 and the third six, for the 66 in 1966. That should have made 6666, but who's counting? I certainly wasn't going to tell the idiot.

When I tried to talk to him about the way he was treating me, it would set him off and he would get crazy. He broke my arm, my ribs, and my spirit. People asked, "Why didn't you leave?" I tried to leave him after my son Patrick was two years old. I traveled to upstate New York to hide, but his father hired detectives to find me and they did. Patrick brought me back, beat me relentlessly until I heard bells and so I stayed for another round of hell. After all, I was Satan's Daughter.

Where Was The Glow?

Pregnant again, I quit the drugs. Doing my best to hide any "glow" of pregnancy as that only increased Patrick's anger. When the "glow" showed, it was a *green light* for Patrick to kick me in the stomach with his steel tipped boots. The "Glow" sent me to the hospital on May 25, 1989, when my second child David, was born pre-mature, only two pounds-four ounces. When I was admitted to the emergency room, I told the truth, even though Patrick had told me to say I tripped and fell down the stairs. The police arrested the son of a bitch, charged him with domestic violence, and put him into a mental ward for a month.

When he was released, he came back with a vengeance.

With two kids, we needed more room. Patrick moved us into a seven-room apartment, also in Brooklyn, around Avenue P. We fixed the place up much better than the one we had lived in when we first got married. It was real pretty and comfortable. I put up cute curtains, we got new furniture and the baby's room was a real nursery. Patrick used one of the other seven rooms for his music, another for his pool table, and a couple of rooms for cutting and packaging drugs. There were people constantly coming in and out of our apartment for drugs. He also had other dealers selling for him, with junkies would banging on our door even at two in the morning. Patrick would push me to answer the door with junkies screaming, "I just want a dime bag." He didn't care who was at the door, he knew it wasn't the police. He was using drugs, so he was pretty careless. His friend, Sonny's brother, was a cop and supplied him with confiscated drugs taken from other drug dealers. Patrick knew the local cops weren't going to mess with him. But things would eventually change when he was no longer their partner.

After David was born, I started using crack again to deal with the beatings, physical and verbal abuse. Then came a time when Patrick, wouldn't let me have any more crack. Was he looking out for me or just didn't want a junky around the kids? Or most likely, my habit was costing him money.

For once he was right, but I was a junky now. I told him I could make my own money and went out on the street wearing a sexy red dress and high heels. I went "Pretty Woman," to get the money I needed for crack. Fortunately, the first car I walked up to was a do-gooder priest. He flipped me out. I asked if he had any money and he said "no," so I just told him to "fuck off" and got out of the car. When I stepped out, the heel on my stilettos broke. I fell and split my knee open. The next car that approached me was a guy named Johnson. He noticed all the tracks on my arm and asked me if I wanted to live the rest of my life like that. At that point, I just broke down crying and said no. He told me he worked for a drug program and he got me admitted into Samarian Village in upstate New York. I went through detox for eight weeks. I got cleaned up and never did it again. While in detox, my sister Theresa took care of my boys.

Joe and Sister Theresa

Teresa, Gloria's sister, is a sweet, sweet woman, who gave birth to three children who grew up to live normal lives.

Theresa did tell me that she'd defended Gloria by jumping on Patrick's back, pulling his hair and digging her nails into his face when he was punching, kicking and dragging Gloria by the hair while she was pregnant. Her story confirmed the physical abuse Gloria suffered and why she finally snapped.

My Life Savers

It was becoming scary clear to me that I wasn't as strong as Tina Turner. Suicide seemed to be the only way to escape my life of all the verbal and physical abuse. My children were the only thing holding me back, from checking out.

On August 6, 1990, I was given another reason to live—my son Dominic, was born. In celebration of his birth, Patrick's mother, hoping to encourage her son Patrick to change his life and to provide a better environment for her grandchildren, gave us a beautiful $300,000 three story house in Gerritsen Beach, Brooklyn. Our home was in a private community, surrounded by water. But it failed to stop the drugs and it didn't stop the slapping, kicking, punching and all the other violence that goes hand in hand with domestic violence. That was the brutality my boys had to witness.

Eventually, with the destructive environment continuing, his parents persuaded him to let me go for the sake of their grandchildren. They knew he was bad, but he was their son. Patrick agreed after his father told him that he wasn't going to help him anymore if he got arrested on another count of domestic violence.

The Divorce

I was once told that my marriage to Patrick was like a person who purchases a boat. The first happiest day in my life was the day I married Patrick. The second happiest day in my life was when I was twenty-three and I divorced the mother fucker. Unfortunately, because of the drugs and all the mental and physical abuse, I was certified mentally unfit to take care of my kids. Patrick with the help and influence of his family was given custody of my boys. I was allowed limited visitation rights.

During the divorce process I met Cisco and I told a friend, "I'm going to marry that man" and I did. He treated me really good, he loved me and showed it. Experiencing kindness, made me realize the wrongness of Patrick's behavior. I now knew whenever I saw my children that I would be subject to his moods and potential cruelty and it terrified me.

Together, Cisco and I started a carnival side show. We sold photos of kids next to cartoon characters. We wore costumes of Barney and Baby Bop. We also had a game where you had to be able to throw a ball into a basket game and we also sold T shirts. We sometimes made as much as $4,000 in a single day—legally and without hurting a soul.

Cisco hated Patrick for what he did to me, what he did to the kids and for what he represented. Patrick resented Cisco, blaming Cisco for my leaving and giving me the strength to stay away from him. Cisco told Patrick he would kill him if he ever harmed or tried to hurt me or the kids. For my protection, Cisco took me to Florida for a vacation, were we went to firing ranges and practiced shooting.

Unfortunately, I eventually left Cisco when I learned he started doing crack. I wasn't going to live that nightmare again, but that was after the *day the music died*.

The Day the Music Died

March 12, 1991, I was no longer controlled by Patrick. I wanted to be a better person and self-sufficient. I was attending nursing school when I shot Patrick. I still loved him and I hated him. I didn't want to kill him, but I just snapped.

My mother said I deserved a medal. I know now that I put myself in that situation and it was my fault as well for allowing it to happen. Why didn't I listen to those that loved me? I guess I needed to learn the hard way—sad but true.

The cops weren't fond of Patrick any longer, in fact, they really hated him. He was always getting arrested and generally never spent a night in jail, getting right back on the street. Whenever the police came to our apartment on a domestic violence call, they said, "One day, one of you is going to kill the other." Who was going to kill who first was the only question?

After the divorce, my three sons lived with Patrick in the home we'd shared before the divorce. On the day I shot Patrick, my son Patrick Jr. called me. I only saw my boys on the weekends. At that time, Patrick Jr. was eleven, David—five, and Dominic—four.

On March 12, 1994, Patrick Jr. called and told me I needed to get over to the house. "We didn't have any food or anything to drink for the last two days and the babies got blood on their bottoms and Dad is running around with this black girl, smoking crack." I can't prove that he was sexually abusing my kids, but I knew if my kids stayed with him, in time they would be abused, raped or killed.

Knowing I had to go there, knowing he was on crack, I wasn't going without a gun. I took my husband Cisco's 380 caliber, silver gun with a pearl handle while he was in the shower. He didn't know I took it and never admitted to the police that it was his gun.

Before I went to Patrick's house to take care of my kids, I called my friend Jessy Rose and asked her to go there, before I got there. I told her I could kill Patrick, for what he was doing to the kids. Cisco had also been pushing me, afraid that as long as Patrick was alive, I was at risk. He wanted him dead. He told me, "If you love me, you'll kill him."

Jessy Rose said she would shoot him, because she also hated him for what he was and what he had done to me. We had known each other since we were kids. I insisted if anyone was going to do it, I would be the one. We decided that Jessy Rose would try to seduce him and then start screaming rape - a lie, but that was what we would tell the police. Then I would come to her rescue and do what had to be done. That was the plan.

Jessy Rose was nervous when she entered Patrick's house with a bottle of Jack Daniels. I got there shortly after she did and cleaned my babies up. I was wearing high heel boots, tight jeans, a little mini top and a long fur coat. If you're going to be getting a mug shoot, why not make sure your picture looks better than your passport photo.

I believe my boys were in the den playing. Upstairs in Patrick's bedroom, he had already stripped naked and had Jessy Rose on the bed, ripping her clothes off and was actually going to rape her. He then came at me. I closed my eyes and started shooting and didn't stop until the gun clicked empty. There was no need to frame him when I shot him eight times, *see you in hell*. I never thought killing him would improve my chance of getting into heaven.

The police said, I managed to hit every one of Patrick's vital body organs. I guess practice makes perfect. After I shot him, I wouldn't go back up to the bedroom— just in case he was still alive. If there was a breath left in his body, I would be dead. So, I sent my oldest son Patrick, to make sure he was dead. I knew Patrick wouldn't hurt him. My poor son, I'm sorry he had to go through that. I later learned that he was in the other room when I shot him. He was peeking through the door. He saw and heard everything. Thank you, Jesus, he was never called as a witness. My poor son. I can still hear his screams when he saw his father's body riddled with bullets and covered in blood.

I called the police and that was the story, I told the detectives. I told the truth. They were probably pleased since Patrick had a long rap sheet. As they were taking me away in handcuffs, the radio was playing our song, "Seasons in the Sun" by Terry Jacks. "Goodbye my love, it's time to die," I broke down crying like a baby. I couldn't believe what I'd done. I killed someone I once loved and now I'm going away for a long, long time. At least, that's what I thought. Although, I would do it again to save my babies.

March 13, I'm Indicted

The day after I shot Patrick, two things happened. First, I learned that once my sisters heard that I killed Patrick, they were all driving up from Florida to support me. Second, I was indicted (officially charged by the police) for Murder in the Second Degree and Criminal Possession of a weapon in the second degree & Criminal Possession of illegal weapon in the third degree.

Following is a copy of the actual indictment presented to the court.

CRIMINAL COURT OF THE CITY OF NEW YORK
PART APAR COUNTY OF KINGS

```
                                          >
    THE PEOPLE OF THE STATE OF NEW YORK    >
                                          >                STATE OF NEW YORK
                   v.                      >                COUNTY OF KINGS
                                          >
         GLORIA DELAURENTIS                >
                                          >
              DEFENDANT                     >
                                          >
```

DET. ROBERT MOORE OF 61 SQD, SHIELD 3449 SAYS THAT ON OR ABOUT
   MARCH 12, 1994 AT APPROXIMATELY 5:15PM AT AN FLORENCE AVE , COUNTY OF
   KINGS, STATE OF NEW YORK,

        THE DEFENDANT COMMITTED THE OFFENSES OF:
        PL 125.25-1   MURDER IN THE SECOND DEGREE
        PL 265.03   CRIMINAL POSSESSION OF A WEAPON IN THE SECOND
                             DEGREE AFO

IN THAT THE DEFENDANT DID: INTENTIONALLY CAUSE THE DEATH OF A
PERSON AND POSSESS A LOADED FIREARM WITH THE INTENT TO USE IT
UNLAWFULLY.

                                                   94K014123

THE SOURCE OF DEPONENT'S INFORMATION AND THE GROUNDS FOR DEPONENT'S
BELIEF ARE AS FOLLOWS:

        THE DEPONENT IS INFORMED BY DEFENDANT'S OWN STATEMENTS THAT, AT
THE ABOVE TIME AND PLACE, THE DEFENDANT DID WITH INTENT OF CAUSING
THE DEATH OF PATRICK DELAURENTI, SHOOT PATRICK DELAURENTI CAUSING HIS
DEATH.
        DEPONENT IS FURTHER INFORMED BY P.O. FRAN LAURIA OF THE 61ST
PRECINCT THAT DEFENDANT DID POSSESS A LOADED .380 CALIBER HANDGUN IN
THAT INFORMANT DID RECOVER SAID HANDGUN ON DEFENDANT'S PERSON.

                              FALSE STATEMENTS MADE IN THIS DOCUMENT ARE
                              PUNISHABLE AS A CLASS A MISDEMEANOR PURSUANT
                              TO SECTION 210.45 OF THE PENAL LAW.

                   3/13/94   Det Robt E Moore 3407
                   DATE   SIGNATURE

mlm

44

March 13 Video Transcript

Following, are two transcripts, one by the detective who arrested Gloria, and the other by Gloria and Detective Moore. I posted them both as there are some discrepancies in her story of the events, on The Day the Music Died.

March 13, 1994 - in a court document, Detective Robert Moore stated the following: On March 12, 1994 at approximately 5:15PM at 65 Florence Ave. Brooklyn, The defendant Gloria De Laurentis committed the offense of MURDER IN THE SECOND DEGREE, CRIMINAL POSSESSION OF A WEAPON IN THE SECOND DEGREE. And, that Gloria De Laurentis, intentionally caused the death of a person and possessed a loaded firearm with the intent to use it unlawfully. He further stated that Gloria De Laurentis own statement; did with intent cause the death of Patrick De Laurentis, causing his death.

The following is the actual, word for word, transcription, of the accounts by Detective Moore.

"Mrs. De Laurentis states that she was called early on the morning of 3/12/94, by her ex-husband Patrick who told her that a pipe had burst in her son's room and she had to come over right away. When she arrived at his house, at 68 Florence Avenue, Patrick Sr. was not there. Since the place was a mess she and her kids began to clean up. A while later Patrick arrived with a black woman named "Pat" whom Gloria described as a drug dealer. Patrick told her that if she gave him $20 for crack he would do that and then stop, so she gave it to him. He then went upstairs with the woman. She called her friend Jessie and asked her to come over because Patrick was acting crazy. The black woman then asked her to call her a taxi so she could leave and she did so. She stated that she stole a gun from her boyfriend three or four days before, and had kept it in her coat since then and on 3/12/94, she took it with her to her husband's house, and that she showed it to him at the point and he tried to take it from her so she pointed it at him. When her friend Jessie arrived, Patrick said that he wanted some alcohol, so Jessie went out and got some Blackberry Brandy. She said that she and Jessie each had about 3 or 4 cups and Patrick drank the rest. He then asked if he could talk to Jessie in private, and she agreed. They went upstairs. She then heard Jesse screaming so she went upstairs. She yelled at Patrick and he yelled back that he would kill her. He was on top of Jessie, but he turned towards her and was moving toward her when she shot him. She stated that she shot once and saw that it hit Patrick, then closed her eyes and kept shooting, she's not sure how many shots. She stated that Jessie was still in the room when she shot Patrick. <u>She then went down and called 911</u>. She then sent Jessie up to check on

Patrick and she said he seemed okay. The police arrived soon thereafter."

The following is a second transcript that includes Gloria's own words in response to question by Detective Moore, as well as comments by Detective Moore. You may find that it differs slightly from her responses given in the interview and those given to me in the writing of this story.

1.)"*My husband (Patrick De Laurentis) was babbling. The gun was mine 1 brought it here.*" Gloria De Laurentis then related the following events that led to shooting. At approximately 0715hrs this date her husband Patrick De Laurentis from whom she was divorced from for one year, called her at her apartment, 4807 Surf Ave #12, and stated to her "*you better come over, a pipe broke in the boys room, I need your help. If you don't come, you'll have trouble seeing the kids again.*" Mrs.

De Laurentis stated that her husband (ex) had custody of their three sons, Patrick M/W/11, David M/W/5, and Dominick M/W/4. She arrived at the residence, 68 Florence Ave between 0900hrs and 0930hrs. Her boyfriend Cisco drove her there. When she arrived, she found her three sons' home by themselves. The son said their father was out all night. About an hour later (1000hrs-1030hrs) Patrick De Laurentis came home in the company of a black woman who sold crack to Patrick. Mrs. De Laurentis did not know the woman's name.

When Patrick arrived home, he was high. Patrick told Gloria to give him money so he could buy more drugs. Mrs. De Laurentis stated she gave him $20.00 more crack and the black woman and Patrick sat in the kitchen and smoked it. During this time, Patrick was acting irrational and kept pulling his penis out of his pants and playing with himself and jerking off, in front of the kids. At some point, the black woman asked to leave and a PDQ car service was called. Patrick continued to act in a crazy manner and kept stating that someone was going to kill him, and he must kill before it happens. At this point Patrick is roaming around the house nude from waist down.

2.) Mrs. De Laurentis continued: At approximately 1230hrs-1300hrs, she called Cousin Jesse Rose and requested that she come over to help try and control Patrick. She has known Jesse most of her life and considers her a cousin. Jesse arrived at the home about 1400hrs and they decided that Jesse would go get some Blackberry Brandy and some Potato Chips and see if this would calm Patrick down. All this time, Mrs. DeLaurentis tried to get Patrick to go to bed, but he refused and continued to rant and rave. When Jesse returned, they along with Patrick were smoking marijuana and drinking the Brandy in the kitchen with Patrick while he continued to play with himself.

3.) At a point in time, unspecified by Mrs. De Laurentis, she was unable to convince Patrick to go upstairs and try to sleep. Patrick, however while upstairs continued to act wild. Jesse Rose told Mrs. De Laurentis that she would go upstairs and try and calm him down. After a few minutes, Mrs. De Laurentis heard Jesse screaming and went upstairs to help Jesse. When she got to the bedroom, she could see Patrick on top of Jesse "*raping her*." Mrs. DeLaurentis', who had the gun (. 380 Davis Automatic) in her waistband, took the gun out and started shooting. Mrs. De Laurentis stated she was in the entrance to the bedroom. She then went downstairs and called 911.

4.) At this point in the interview, I asked Mrs. De Laurentis to show me and tell me again where she was standing and what transpired when she got to the bedroom. Mrs. De Laurentis stated, she heard Jesse screaming and she went upstairs to help her. She had the gun, in her waistband. When she' got to the bedroom doorway, she could see Patrick on top of Jesse. She screamed, Patrick turned around and got off of Jesse, standing on the fair side of the bed. Patrick states to Gloria "*You are the daughter of Satan*." You have to die." With that, Patrick came at Mrs. De Laurentis and she stated, "*I started to shoot, I kept shooting*." <u>She then ran downstairs and shouted call 911</u>.

After the initial videotaping of her confession, she was sent to Riker's Island Prison, New York.

March 14, 1994

**Two days after I killed the father of my kids, a legal aid attorney, Elizabeth Ramsey was assigned my case. Up to that point, I was told my rights, and did not ask to lawyer up. Ms. Ramsey was later replaced Lisa Schriebersdorf to whom I owe my life and my liberty.

On March 24, 1994, I was arraigned in front of a judge and formally charged with Murder in the Second Degree and one count of criminal possession and one count of illegal use of a loaded firearm. Following is a copy of my arraignment document.

COUNTY OF KINGS
------------------------------------X
THE PEOPLE OF THE STATE OF NEW YORK

OFFICE OF THIS
District Attorney
CHARLES J. HYNES
DISTRICT ATTORNEY

-against-

1. Gloria Delmonte

2. _____

Docket/Indictment # 3098/94

Docket/Indictment # _____

Defendant(s)
------------------------------------X

Form prepared by: A.D.A. ANDREW J. LAUER   Date: 3/14/94

Form served by: _____ /Upon: _____ Date: _____

NOTICES

I.(A) PLEASE TAKE NOTICE that, pursuant to CPL 240.20(1)(a), statements in the form noted below were made by the defendant or by a co-defendant to be tried jointly, other than in the course of the criminal transaction, to a public servant engaged in law enforcement activity or to a person then acting under the direction or in cooperation with such public servant.

	Def.#	Date	Time Appar.	Place	Person to Whom Made
1. Written: (a)					
(b)					
2. Stenographic: (a)	1	3/8/94	3.00pm	Kings Cnty Crml Ct	Grad Jury
(b)					
3. Audio tape: (a)					
(b)					
4. Video tape: (a)	1	3/13/94	1.00pm	61 pct.	ADA Chudebol
(b)					
5. Oral Statements: (a)	1	3/12/94	5.15pm	61 Flores Avenue	P.O. Lewin
(b)	1	3/12/94	6.10pm	61 Flores Avenue	Det. Robert Moore

Substance of oral statement (Specify defendant #): PEDEGREE INFORMATION;

(a) I shot my husband, his upstairs. I have the gun in my wristband; the gun was here & she bought it because she was afraid of deceased; she carried gun because she had been raped in the past.
(4a) & (5b) See attached.

(B) PLEASE TAKE FURTHER NOTICE that, pursuant to CPL 710.30(1)(a), the People intend to offer evidence of the above statement(s) of the defendant(s) on the People's direct case at the trial of this action, except for the statements specified above in paragraph(s)_____.

(C) A transcript of any stenographically recorded statement or a copy of any written statement are either appended or will be made available to counsel at a mutually convenient time. A copy of any electronically recorded statement will be provided counsel following receipt of an appropriate blank type cartridge.

ECAB-22a

54

From Murder to Manslaughter

On March 30, 1994, the District Attorney, Charles J Hynes informed the court that the Prosecution was ready for trial. However, on April 1, 1994, District Attorney, Charles J. Hynes, reduced the initial indictment against me from Murder in the Second Degree to Manslaughter in the First Degree; stating that "the circumstances do not constitute murder as defendant was under extreme disturbance..." The charges of Criminal Possession of a weapon in the Second Degree & Criminal Possession of illegal weapon in the Third Degree remained as initially charged. If convicted, I would still be looking at many years in prison.

While imprisoned at Riker's Island, awaiting trial, my family brought me some jeans and sneakers to replace my dress and stilettos. There was a gym at Riker's Island. Every day I spent hours walking and running up and down the bleachers praying, "Dear God, if you had a plan for me, I'm sure I screwed it up. I hope you haven't given up on me. I didn't want to kill him, but I did, but if you think I deserve another chance to do right by my kids, I promise, I'll be the best person I can. Please God, help me."

I remained at Ricker's Island for approximately another two months until my next appearance in front of the judge. Every day, I relived the day the music died for me.

Released on My Own Recognizance

May 20, 1994, I was at Riker's Island for a
little over two months and had no clue of what God
had decided would be my fate. However, my charge
of Murder in the Second Degree had been reduced
to Manslaughter in the Second Degree. My new
attorney, Lisa Schrieberdorf, came by to let me
know that she'd filed a motion for discovery and a
motion to suppress information that could be
damaging to my case.

The good news, on June 12, 1994, I was
scheduled to go in front of the judge for bail
reduction so I could get out and see my boys.

On the day I went before the judge, I was in
tears as I entered the courtroom. The judge stared
straight at me. My attorney was going over my file
with the prosecutor and the judge. I don't know if
the judge and prosecutor felt sorry for me, or if they
were just glad that a child molester and drug dealer
was no longer on the street, and no longer able to

57

create terror and menace innocent children. Whatever, I was in shock when the judge announced I was going to be released on my own recognizance (zero bail money) until my trial, which might be months away. Jesus must have heard my prayers. Thank you, Jesus. And thank you Lisa Schrieberdorf.

I was, for now, free until my trial, or until Patrick's father had me killed, which I understood was his intention.

October 3rd. 1994 Patrick's Mother's Letter in His Defense

Approximately, four months passed. I was unable to see my kids and I had been hiding out because of threats on my life. I learned, some of Patrick's defenders were trying to make me out as the bad guy. Lisa Schrieberdorf provided me with the first letter sent to the judge by Patrick's mother, now my ex mother-in-law. Following is that letter. I guess it's my word, against hers.

Oct 3, 1994 Letter to: Judge Douglas,

Your Honor,

I'm a broken hearted mother who lost her only son. I grieve for my son every day. He didn't deserve such a violent death and in his own bedroom nevertheless! He was raising three young boys. He was always there for them. He had to have his former wife removed from his home in May of

59

1991. She was put in a mental hospital in Coney Island. <u>She threatened his life many times, but mostly with a knife. She even stabbed him a few times, but he refused to press charges</u>. She was very violent to her children. I had one of their sons living with me. To let her go without serving a jail sentence is a travesty of the law. She went to his home and threatened him with a loaded gun to murder him.

She didn't belong in that house. She lived with her boyfriend. She accused my son of battery when she was the one who hit and hurt him. I fear for her children. She's not capable of dealing with them. She was found unfit in 1991 and Judge awarded the children to their father. She crushed their poor kid's hearts, who grieve for their father. She broke all our hearts. My son was an underdog. He loved her and paid a big penalty for it. I now live in Florida and I'm under a doctor's care for my grief and nerves. I can't even travel, I'm too grief stricken. Please incarcerate her and have them put under mental care. This woman is sick and full of violence. Please try to protect my grandchildren. The children were all cocaine babies. She took drugs when she was pregnant. The children are all in Special Classes. Please help them your honor.

Sincerely,

Mrs. De Laurentis

October 13, 1994 - Women's Prison
Letter to Court

By October 13, 1994, it was obvious, I
wasn't going to get any support from Patrick's
family, but fortunately the Women's Prison
Association requested that I be entered into The
Transitional Residence Program. Following is that
letter.

> *The Women's Prison Association &*
> *Home Inc.*
> 110 Second Avenue. New York, New
> York 10003.

October 13, 1994

Honorable Justice Douglas

Brooklyn County Supreme Court

360 Adams Street, Part 9

Brooklyn, N Y 11201

Dear Justice Douglas:

I am writing to you on behalf of Ms. Gloria De Laurentis who was referred to the Hopper Home Alternative-to-Incarceration (ATI) Program by Ms. Judith Rhodes of the Legal Aid Society. Ms. De Laurentis was interviewed, and after careful consideration and verification of the information gathered we found her eligible for our Reporting Program. Since Hopper Home is a fairly new program please allow me to provide you with a brief overview of the services and supervision we provide at the Women's Prison Association.

Since 1844, The Women's Prison Association (WPA) has assisted women in their role as mothers and caretakers. From establishing the first halfway house and vocational training program for women in the country, to developing a program to aid pregnant offenders, the WPA has been in the forefront of providing services for women and their families.

Hopper Home, a project of WPA offers the Court system an ATI composed of two modalities, residential and reporting. Hopper Home is a drug-free, safe environment, with 24-hour supervision. The Transitional Residence program consists of 16 beds, created for jail bound, homeless women who would not be eligible to participate in an ATI without a residential component. The Reporting component is a six months program designed for women who can live in their own residence, and are at risk of incarceration or detained. Reporting clients are required to attend Hopper Home a minimum of three times per week.

Upon entering Hopper Home, women are assigned a case planner who conducts an enhanced assessment, and develops a program to service her individual needs. Residents and reporting clients must attend on-site groups and workshops which are conducted by experts in the areas of substance abuse, parenting, independent living skills, women's health issues, HIV/AIDS awareness to name a few. Moreover, all clients must provide urine samples for drug testing three times weekly. Hopper Home is also contracted by the Child Welfare Agency (CWA) to provide eligible clients with Preventive Services which is designed to reunite and preserve families. In addition to these services, Hopper Home assists women in filing for and receiving benefits, and attaining appropriate housing.

I hope the above provides your Honor with an idea about the type of services Hopper can offer to Ms. Gloria De Laurentis. If your Honor would consider Hopper Home's reporting program as an ATI for Gloria De Laurentis, it is our policy to provide the courts with progress reports and to notify the courts of any changes in a client's supervision status.

Ms. De Laurentis could truly benefit from the services provided by the Hopper Home Reporting program. We would provide her with our preventive services as well as assistance with housing in conjunction with referrals for therapy and any other necessary programs. I appreciate your consideration and interest in this matter.

Sincerely, Ann L. Jacobs
Intake Coordinator

cc: Lisa Schrieber-Stdorf, Esq.
Judith Rhodes

Jacobs *Executive* Re: Gloria De Laurentis

Memories, Gloria Goes to Live with Her Father

Having to fill in some blanks in Gloria's story, she and her sister Tracy came to my home. My first question to Gloria was, "How did she feel about her father? How did she feel about him being a millionaire and giving Ashley preferential treatment? Did she resent Ashley living in a mansion, growing up with a nanny and being showered with money when she needed it?

Gloria just looked at me with a smile on her face, then burst out laughing. "She told you that story? Ashley is delusional. She didn't live in a mansion and she wasn't raised with a nanny."

Still shaking my head, "So, she didn't live in a mansion?" I had to wait a couple of minutes for Gloria to stop laughing. Finally.

"As far as I was concerned, my father was a rotten bum. He worked as a bus driver and janitor in

New Jersey and never provided any financial or emotional support, nor did he show any interest in seeing me, Theresa or Tracey."

Thinking for a moment, "You knew about the stories, didn't you confront her?"

"Sure, but she would just shrug her shoulders and turn away. Ashley is our sister. We love her, we accepted her."

"Gloria, did you ever go to live with your father and Ashley?"

"When I was eleven, I went to live with my father in New Jersey. It was a horrible experience: My father's girlfriend was jealous of my father's attention to me, which wasn't much, and she used a bat to bust the windshield on his car. After that he put me on a bus home to my mother."

Tracey, listening, couldn't wait to speak. "Theresa and I, at one point, thought it would be nice to live with our father and Ashley - big mistake. The place was a three-room shack. There was no running water, newspaper for wallpaper, an outhouse, and a blanket for our bedroom door. For one month, we ate nothing but macaroni every day until we decided to go home. We never spoke or heard from our father again.

November 2, 1994 - Request for Protective Custody

By November Gloria was still free, her trial date still unconfirmed, but she continued to be frightened for her life. Therefore, her attorney, Lisa Schriebersdorf, requested that the court provide her with protective custody.

SUPREME COURT OF THE STATE OF NEW YORK
COUNTY OF KINGS: CRIMINAL TERM
——————————————————————————————X

THE PEOPLE OF THE STATE OF NEW YORK, :

                    Plaintiff,   **AFFIRMATION**

    -against-   :   Indict. # 3098/94

GLORIA DELAURENTIS,

                    Defendant.   :
——————————————————————————————X

STATE OF NEW YORK)
) ss.:
COUNTY OF KINGS   )

        LISA SCHREIBERSDORF, an attorney at law and associated with
ROBERT M. BAUM, Esq., the attorney of record for the defendant,
hereby affirms and states:

        1. On October 14, 1994, the defendent was ordered to be
housed in protective custody by Justice Douglass. However, as
of November 1, 1994 the defendent has not been placed in
protective custody.

        2. The defendant is in fear of physical injury. Therefore,
the defendant request placement in Protective Custody.

        WHEREFORE, the defendant requests that the Court issue an
Order directing the Department of Corrections to house the
defendant in Protective Custody and to take any appropriate means
to insure her safety.

Dated: Brooklyn, New York
       November 2nd, 1994

                                        Lisa Sche
                                        —————————————————
                                        LISA SCHREIBERSDORF

November 2, 1994 - Court Ordered Protection

On the same day, Gloria was granted Protective Custody.

At a Criminal Term, Part 9 of the Supreme Court of the State of New York, held in and for the County of Kings, at the Courthouse thereof, 360 Adams Street, Brooklyn, New York, on the 2nd day of November, 1994.

PRESENT:

HONONRABLE   LEWIS L. DOUGLASS
                    JUSTICE
---X

THE PEOPLE OF THE STATE OF NEW YORK,   **ORDER**

                    Plaintiff,   :

        -against-   :   INDICT. # 1009793
                                                    3028-94
GLORIA DELAURENTIS,   :

                    Defendant.
---X

TO THE WARDEN: ROSE M. SINGER CENTER
                      19-19 HAZEN STREET
                      EAST ELMHURST, NEW YORK 11370

and any other New York City or State Correctional Institution who

has custody of **Gloria Delaurentis**, Book & Case # 110-94-00788;

NYSID # 7623481M, it is hereby

        Ordered, that defendant **Gloria Delaurentis** be housed in a

Correctional Institution under **Protective Custody**.

                    E N T E R,

                                            Douglass J.S.C.
        ENTERED   JUSTICE, SUPREME COURT

        NOV 3 1994

        WILBUR A. LEVIN
        COUNTY CLERK

November 9, 1994
Guilty Plea Proposed

On November 9, 1994, Attorney, Lisa
Shriebersdorf, proposed a guilty plea to reduce the
charges one more time. The first time, it was
reduced from Murder in the Second Degree to
Manslaughter in the First Degree and now,
hopefully it would be reduced to Manslaughter in
the Second Degree, with a proposed sentence of six
months in jail and five years' probation. That was
the proposal, although the prosecution would have
to accept the deal and that wasn't guaranteed.

Until then, Gloria's attorney was building
her case. And, those who loved Patrick, were
presenting Gloria in a different light - a much
darker light.

November 14, 1994 Patrick's Girlfriend's Letter to Court

On November 14, 1994, Patrick's girlfriend, Janet Brennan wrote a letter that was forwarded to Judge Douglas. (Mrs. Corbin was assisting the public defender at the time)

Dear Mrs. Corbin,

I met you in court while you were protecting Gloria De Laurentis, she killed her ex-husband and was awaiting trial. This letter is to inform you that she is one of those women who used your agency. She claimed she was a battered wife and that's why she had to kill him in COLD BLOOD with seven bullets.

I was on the phone with him until 5:03 P.M., he was extremely tired and was going to sleep. At 5:11 pm, the police were called that he was dead. Gloria claimed that raping and beating her girlfriend (she

74

now admits that she lied). She bragged to her son "with her record she will be off in a few months" and will take the kids to Florida.

Patrick De Laurentis was a good father and kind to Gloria. The incidents of fights were over four years in the past. He let her in his house out of his own kindness to let her visit the kids. She never really showed much interest in them. Only as an excuse to visit Pat, as she knew, he always has a love for her and she could manipulate him.

Instead of being punished for her evil, she was pampered by your agency and judge who believed she was "a victim". This girl spent her life robbing men for drug money, she prostitutes etc., and steals at any opportunity.

Patrick De Laurentis, although still addicted to drugs, fought to get off, helped other people, was honest and decent. He loved and cared for his kids with all his heart. She is a drug addict, but judged him and decided he should die for it.

Now she is pleading to get 6 months and then will take her kids. She never even changed a diaper for them and now she wants to remove the kids from his sister's home where they are safe.

As his girlfriend, I seen his love and his growth. This is a terrible injustice, because of his death, all the people he helped are being deprived, his children, parents, family and me. Yet she drives in a new Cadillac and is protected by agencies like yours. I had to write to tell you, you've been had. I have to now do a campaign to warn people that woman are killing men and hiding behind "Wife Beating" agencies.

Many news agencies will get this letter. I was horrified to see you "Mrs. Corbin" a sincere great lady protect and coddle a cold blooded killer who should have been punished, not coddled. She really had your agency. It is out of Love for a kind decent man that I worked hard to better his life and that is why I must write this letter and do something about agencies protecting Cold Blooded Woman who use wife beating as an excuse.

Sincerely Yours,
Janet Brennan
(Copy to Judge Douglas)

November 25, 1994
Attorney's Arguments for Battered Women

The following document presented to the court included arguments presented by Gloria's attorney Lisa Schreibersdorf, to show that Gloria De Laurentis defense was not "Battered Women's Syndrome," which in the past was connected to an insanity plea, due to constant physical and mental abuse.

The following also describes how over the past years the courts and society have traditionally treated women differently than men regarding abuse and rape by husbands. I have shortened or eliminated some text that I felt was repetitious.

No matter if one believed Gloria intentionally killed her husband or not, she lived under the constant threat that she would be killed.

My personal thoughts as I read and learned, I wondered why so many judges sided with men who abused women, was that possibly many of those judges were as guilty as the men they protected. Just a guess.

If you are a woman in an abusive relationship, before taking action be sure to read the following legal arguments presented in Gloria DeLaurentis's case.

Supreme COURT OF THE STATE OF NEW YORK
County OF KINGS

--------------------------------X

THE PEOPLE OF THE STATE OF NEW YORK
IND. # 3098/94

AFFIRMATION IN

OPPOSITION TO MOTION

-against-

GLORI DE LAURENTIS,

----- ----------------------------------x

STATE OF NEW YORK)

) SS:

COUNT OF KINGS)

LISA SCHREIBERSDORF, an attorney-at-law associated with ROBERT M. BAUM, the assigned counsel for the defendant, does hereby affirm the following statement to be true under penalty of perjury.

The defendant is currently charged with Manslaughter 1°, Criminal Possession of a weapon 2°, and Criminal Possession of a Weapon 3°.

The criminal charges arise from the shooting by Ms. De Laurentis of her estranged husband Patrick De Laurentis.

Ms. De Laurentis has been subjected to extreme physical and emotional abuse at the hands of the decedent over the course of many years.

The defense will assert at the trial of this matter that Ms. De Laurentis was justified in shooting her ex-husband based on an imminent threat to her and other people present in the home that day.

In Support of the defense, it will be crucial that Ms. Laurentis describe past behavior of the decedent to explain her reasonable belief that he was dangerous at the moment she shot him.

The defense does not intend to interpose an insanity defense or assert in any way that Ms. De Laurentis was not responsible for her action.

The defense does intend, however, with leave of this court to call Dr. Mary Ann Dutton as an expert witness. Dr has not interviewed Gloria De

81

Laurentis, nor will she with speak with Ms. De Laurentis prior to the trial. Dr. Dutton will testify in general terms about the effect of long term battering upon the psyche of the one being battered. She will also describe in general the typical behaviors displayed by "battered women" which may be counter intuitive. For Example, Dr. Dutton can describe the phenomenon whereby battered women voluntarily return to the abusive spouse after the abuse. Dr. Dutton will be asked about other common traits which women who have been abused may display such as coldness and manipulative behavior, which may be misread by a jury uneducated in the cause and effect in these relationships.

Dr. Sutton will not diagnose Gloria De Laurentis as suffering from "Battered Woman Syndrome." In fact, Dr. Dutton will stats that the diagnosis of a battered woman as having a "syndrome" is not helpful; when evaluating the woman's actions and responses......

It is the defense assertion that this information will be helpful to the jury in determining the reasonableness of Gloria De Laurentis' actions in this instance. The defense will not argue that Gloria De Laurentis suffers from "Battered Women's Syndrome" or that she is impaired or less responsible because of the history between her and the decedent. Quite to the contrary, it is the defendant's claim that given her history, she was the person most acutely aware of the likely behavior of the decedent. Thus, while to an uneducated jury, Ms. De Laurentis may seem to have overacted, in fact, she was responding to actual stimuli that she alone was most likely to see and recognize. It is hoped that Dr. Dutton's testimony can help the jury understand this phenomenon.

Defense Argument

Following are excerpts of lengthy history of prejudice presented to the court in her defense, which helped determine her sentence.

I. In 1982, the law included evidence of a mental disease or deficit to be offered by defense in connection with (1) the defense of lack of criminal responsibility, (2) the defense of extreme emotional disturbance, and (3) any other defense...

II. <u>Testimony on the battered women throughout the country has been prejudiced against them, that juror will not be able to overcome their biases without testimony of expert witnesses to dispel the myths and misconceptions.</u>

Therefore, Ms. De Laurentis's defense will simply be self-defense. That is, the defendant argues that her use of force was justified because she reasonably believed that the decedent was about to inflict serious bodily injury upon her. The law permits her to respond with deadly force in certain circumstances.

The sole difference between this case and more classic notions of self-defense is that the defendant is a woman who has been a long-term victim of battering by the deceased. At trial she may introduce testimony from an expert so that a jury will be able to asses if her reaction in responding to the deceased with deadly force was <u>reasonable</u>. The expert will not offer an opinion on the ultimate issue - that is - whether the defendant's state of mind was a reasonable one at the time she killed her husband. Instead, the expert's testimony about battering is critical to enable the jury to fairly reach its own conclusion on this issue. This testimony, long accepted by courts in New York and other jurisdictions, is about a phenomenon known as the "battered woman's syndrome." Despite its nomenclature as a "syndrome" it does not in this instance, describe a "mental disease or defect. " As more fully described below, this testimony is essential to aid the jury in overcoming myths and misconceptions about how "normal" women would behave if beaten and to the jury in assessing what behavior reasonable for in Mrs. De Laurentis' situation. Until a jury is able to overcome common prejudices such as (1)if she really was beaten she would have left, (2)leaving was a reasonable option for her, (3)she must have "asked for it", and (4)rational women do not use violence, they will be unable to assess the reasonableness of her behavior.

Despite numerous advances for women in the culture and the law, it is extremely difficult for most jurors to accept that a woman who kills her abuser acted rationally. An expert assists a jury in explaining why the behavior of an abused woman is normal and rational. It is the antithesis of a "mental disease or defect."

This testimony does not create a separate and unique defense for battered women. Despite public perception, there is no such thing as the Battered Women's Defense. Battered woman are not entitled to a separate defense because they have been battered. They merely have been allowed to present expert testimony on the battered women syndrome so that they begin their defense on a level playing field before the jury, that is, the testimony is permitted to overcome the prejudices and

misconceptions that jurors have when they begin
such a case.

A. <u>Expert Testimony on the Battered
Women's Syndrome Explains How an Abused
Women's Reaction is Rational and Normal</u>

Before a jury can see a woman as
reasonable, they must see her as rational. Expert
testimony about battered woman's syndrome helps
the jury understand that any reasonable person can
find themselves trapped in an abusive relationship.
<u>Designating a woman as "diseased" or "defective"
because she has remained in an abusive relationship
drags us back to a time of the darkness and
ignorance that enabled the abuser by blaming the
victim.</u>
The battered woman's expert deals with
precisely these prejudices and questions -- the very
kind of obstacles that prevent a juror from being
able to fairly consider a woman's act in self-defense.

Such a position contradicts the reality of the expert testimony and feeds into the prejudices confronting women. It should be against the public policy of this state to declare a woman somehow less than normal by virtue of her presence in that relationship.

B. The History of Prejudice Against Women in the Culture

While prejudice against women may have diminished over time, the history of such prejudice is essential to a proper understanding of why jurors still have misconceptions about battered women.

Less than ten years ago it was not a crime in New York for a man to rape his wife. Known as "marital rape" exemption in the law, this startling fact graphically demonstrates the prejudice grounded in centuries of history that denied equality to women in every forum including the courtrooms.

The term "battered women", much like its visibility in the public eye and the courts, is a relatively recent phenomenon. It was not until the 1970's and the advent of the woman's movement when activists demanded greater protection for victims of domestic violence -- that there was any systemic recognition of a problem that had been relegated to a "personal" issue to be dealt with behind closed doors. The term "battered wife" was coined to focus attention on the plight of women subjected to physical, psychological, and sexual abuse by their intimate, partners.

Following the lead of the National Organization for Women, which formed its task force on battered women and household violence in 1975, battered women's service and advocacy groups developed nationwide.

One immediate result of the increased activity on the behalf of battered women was a general rise in public awareness of intra-family violence through news stories and films. In the

wake of shocking reports on women, child, and
sexual abuse, legislatures showed greater
willingness to intervene in family affairs. The
criminalization of domestic abuse soon followed,
and rape laws were redefined in some jurisdictions
to include marital rape.

Until the mid-1980's in New York State,
domestic violence complaints were handled by the
family courts. Family court judges did not have the
jurisdiction to sentence abusers to jail, most often
they acted as arbitrators. By definition, rape could
not occur in a marital relationship in the United
States until the mid-1970s.

To fully appreciate the prejudices that
underlie the acceptance of battered women in our
society, it is essential to ask: How far have we
really come since ancient Rome? Women's status
was first codified which ordered women to obey
their husbands, and husbands to control their wives.
Roman men were responsible for their wives
behavior and were expected to punish them for

committing crimes. A husband was allowed to use reasonable force, including blackening her eye or breaking her nose in disciplining his wife.

Religious and social philosophies of early history recommended regular chastisement of women, as a practice necessary to the woman's well-being, and as a husband's right, emanating from the ownership of his wife and the mastery of his household. Christian doctrine embodied in the New Testament commanded women to be silent and obedient, and accepting of their husband's authority: "Likewise, you wives, be submissive to your husbands."

Neither English nor American common law recognized women as individuals with personal rights and freedoms. Early English law' held that the "wife's duty was to submit and defer to her husband's rule." The English principle of covertures established that a married woman could not own property free from her husband's claim or control. In fact, women themselves were considered properly disposed of if the male 'owner' of the victim was compensated for damage to his 'property'. Marital rape was inconceivable, as wives could not legally refuse their husbands' conjugal rights.

The prevailing belief that women were property and should be subservient to men was exemplified by a 16th century Russian domestic code, which recommended soundly thrashing "disobedient wives...but 'not straight on the face or the ear' since the husband would be sorely disadvantaged should his spouse become deaf , blind, or otherwise incapacitated. 'Keep the whip, and choose carefully where to strike...' In many parts of Europe, a man could even kill his wife without legal penalty, well into the 1600s. <u>By contrast, a wife who killed her husband would be penalized as if she had committed treason, because her act of homicide was considered analogous to murdering the king</u>.

English common law sanctioned wife-beating under the infamous "rule of thumb," which decreed that a man might use a "rod not thicker than his thumb" with which to chastise his wife. This restriction was meant to protect wives from overzealous husbands. American states adopted the rule early in the 1800's in formal recognition of a husband's right to beat his wife.

In the late 19th century, England instituted many social and legal reforms to benefit women. Chief among them were expanding a wife's legal grounds for divorce to include a severe beating by her husband, prohibition of the sale of wives and daughters into prostitution, and abandonment of the practice of imprisoning women for transgression of their wifely duties.

These new standards of civility travelled to America as well, where women were allowed greater freedom to transact business and sign contracts. By the latter part of the 19th century, both the rule and right to beat one's wife were withdrawn by most states. The first court to do so declared that a husband could not "beat a wife with a stick, pull her hair, choke her, spit in her face, or kick her on the floor. By 1910, 35 out of 46 states had passed reform legislation classifying wife-beating as assault, but prevailing belief in the sanctity and virtual inviolability of the family continued to work against women who attempted to obtain legal remedies for abuse by their spouses.

In the twentieth century women made progress usually in single issue causes. It is the battered women's movement that brought the issue to light since the 1970's but the longstanding prejudices still prevailed

For example, women who attempted to press charges against their abusive spouses soon discovered that entrenched 'hands-off' policies of law enforcement agencies and the criminal courts were much harder to change. It was our judicial system, committed to justice that often failed women.

C. Battered Women in Courts

In New York in 1977, a women who was knifed and seriously injured by her husband was forced to prosecute her case in family court, rather than criminal court, despite her stated wish to bring criminal charges. The appellate division found that criminal court was an inappropriate forum in which to resolve family matters because it considered criminal sanctions, which might include imprisonment, to be too harsh for domestic cases.

And in 1986, a Massachusetts judge criticized a woman (Mrs. Dunn) who requested a protective order for "taking up the court's time when it has a lot more serious matters to contend with. When the woman was kidnapped and murdered by her estranged husband six months later, the chief district court judge showed "contempt for (the Massachusetts) abuse prevention act and gave his opinion that these (were) matters to be resolved within the marital relationship.

(In the above case, the judge was criticized after the woman's death. Boston Globe, Sept. 12, 1986: Dunn was accosted by her estranged husband as she waited at a bus stop with her mother. He sprayed the mother with mace, shot Dunn in the abdomen, then kidnapped her. Dunn was found the next morning, battered and dead, face down in mud at the local rubbish dump.)

Battered women who struck back at their abusers found themselves in conflict with an unyielding and unsympathetic legal system. They found that the traditional self-defense doctrine was unavailable to battered women who killed their abusers, because elements of self-defense, as applied, presupposed two men of equal size and fighting experience. The Wanrow case perceived as a major victory for women turned on the failure of the trail court to use feminine pronouns when instructing the jury. Women found themselves moving from a place in society where they had no rights in relationships with their spouses to a position where their "failure" to leave an abusive relationship either meant the abuse wasn't so bad or the woman was at fault for staying the relationship. Therefore, battered women were often forced to defend themselves in homicide cases by pleading insanity, mental disease or defect, or extreme emotional disturbance. In the case of the State vs Wanrow, it stated, "At common law, the modern extreme emotional disturbance (EED) defense was embodied in the defense of provocation of "sudden heat of passion." A defendant was guilty of voluntary manslaughter, rather than murder, if she intentionally killed the victim while in a state of passion, if the passion was caused by adequate provocation, and if the homicidal act occurred before she had reasonable time to cool off.

However, if a battered woman proved she was laboring under a mental disease of defect at the time of the offense, she was not guilty by reason of insanity. The price for her successful defense was often involuntary commitment to a mental facility for an indefinite time. If on the other hand, a woman was unable to meet the standard for mental disease or defect and her alternative theories of defense rejected, she was found guilty as charged. Lawyers representing battered women learned that the defense of mental disease of defect was very difficult to interpose and prove; even if successful, the defendant suffered the social and personal stigma of insanity.

A battered woman who successfully used the defense of extreme disturbance merely reduced her degree of criminal culpability from murder to manslaughter in the first degree. Under common law, this reduction allowed a defendant who acted in the sudden heat of passion, without first brooding over the provoking incident, or having sufficient time to cool off. This "cooling off" time varied by jurisdiction. In common law, very few types of provocation were considered adequate to sustain this defense. One such sanctioned provocation was available only to men: if a man killed his wife or her lover after observing them in the act of committing adultery, he could defend himself on the grounds of extreme emotional disturbance, because adultery was considered the "highest invasion of (the husband's) property," and a killing provoked by this invasion was felt to be vindication of an injustice. The same defense was not allowed by women.

Battered women who killed their abusers benefitted from advances in sociological scholarship on abused women, which emerged during the late 1970s. Earlier attempts to explain the phenomenon of the battered woman had looked to Freudian theory, which surmised that all woman are naturally masochistic, and that battered women stayed in abusive relationships because they enjoyed the violence. This theory was widely debunked by professionals.

Note 1. In some instances women have been confined to mental institutions longer than any sentence the court could or would impose. Still it is more likely that her incarceration in a mental hospital would be short, because the test applied is whether the mental disease or defect renders her a danger to herself or others.

Note 2. The use of the insanity plea has been criticized because it "emphasizes (women's) mental weakness" and a lack of Equal Rights to a Trial. Furthermore, it was argued, "since women are generally viewed as unreasonable even under normal circumstances, a woman trying to establish an insanity defense may be forced to prove she was 'really crazy and hysterical' before jurors will excuse her."

D. Battered Women's Syndrome Testimony is Accepted by The Courts

As a result of this scholarship, battered woman's syndrome began to be recognized in the 1980s by many jurisdictions, allowing introduction of expert testimony on the syndrome for the defense of battered women who killed their abusive partners. The case of Francine Hughes, dramatized

in the movie "The Burning Bed" signaled the end of
an era where women used insanity defense in
circumstances that would warrant a self-defense
plea for a man.

Joe

Comments on Arguments

I hope you found Gloria's attorney's arguments on the prejudices against women as enlightening as I have. The above arguments, don't suggest an open hunting season on abusive men and husbands, but it does provide a door, when no other exists.

December, 1994
Waiver of Right to Appeal

Gloria did not learn her fate until January 25, 1995. Would she get her plea deal for time served, or go to prison and come out an old woman?

Her attorney's proposal to reduce the remaining charge of Manslaughter in the First Degree to Manslaughter in the Second Degree which was accepted by the district attorney, which carried a shorter sentence.

Gloria, initially admitting to murdering her husband, had no problem signing the following waiver agreement as part of Plea Deal. In doing so, it prevented her from appealing the courts sentence if she wasn't happy with the final sentencing.

Following is a copy of the Waiver Agreement agreed to and signed by Gloria.

STATE OF NEW YORK
SUPREME COURT, KINGS COUNTY

PEOPLE OF THE STATE OF NEW YORK, :

             PLAINTIFF   :   WAIVER OF RIGHT TO APPEAL

           V   :   SUPREME COURT
                  :   INDICTMENT # 3098/94

Gloria DeLaurentis

          DEFENDANT   :

THE UNDERSIGNED DEFENDANT HEREBY WAIVES THE RIGHT TO APPEAL ANY PLEA AND SENTENCE. THE UNDERSIGNED EXECUTES THIS WAIVER AFTER BEING ADVISED BY THE COURT OF THE NATURE OF THE RIGHTS BEING WAIVED. THE UNDERSIGNED HAS BEEN ADVISED OF THE RIGHT TO TAKE AN APPEAL (C.P.L. 450.10), TO PROSECUTE THE APPEAL AS A POOR PERSON AND TO HAVE AN ATTORNEY ASSIGNED IN THE EVENT THAT THE UNDERSIGNED IS INDIGENT, AND TO SUBMIT A BRIEF AND/OR ARGUE BEFORE AN APPELLATE COURT ON ANY ISSUES RELATING TO THE CONVICTION AND SENTENCE. THE UNDERSIGNED REPRESENTS THAT THIS WAIVER IS BEING VOLUNTARILY, KNOWINGLY, AND UNDERSTANDINGLY EXECUTED, OF THE DEFENDANT'S OWN FREE WILL.

                                        _____
                                        DEFENDANT

THE UNDERSIGNED ATTORNEY REPRESENTS THAT PRIOR TO THE SIGNING OF THE FOREGOING WAIVER, THE ABOVE-NAMED DEFENDANT WAS FULLY ADVISED OF THE RIGHTS OF A CONVICTED PERSON TO TAKE AN APPEAL UNDER THE LAWS OF THE STATE OF NEW YORK.

THE UNDERSIGNED FURTHER REPRESENTS THAT, IN MY PROFESSIONAL OPINION, THE ABOVE WAIVER BY THE DEFENDANT OF THE RIGHT TO APPEAL WAS VOLUNTARILY, KNOWINGLY, AND UNDERSTANDINGLY MADE AND RECOMMENDS TO THE COURT THAT THE WAIVER BE APPROVED.

                                        _____
                                        COUNSEL FOR DEFENDANT

THE FOREGOING WAIVER WAS EXECUTED IN OPEN COURT BEFORE ME AS THE TRIAL JUSTICE. THE FOREGOING WAIVER WAS READ TO THE DEFENDANT BY ME.

                            Hon. Lewis Douglass J.S.C.
                            TRIAL JUSTICE

                                    ADM 26 - 10/92

104

The Sentencing

My heart was pounding as I waited for the judge to enter the court room. I sat silently next to my attorney. I had already signed a waiver of my rights to an appeal and a reduced charge of Manslaughter in the Second Degree which was accepted by the District Attorney. All my sisters where there praying along with me.

As we waited, the district attorney and his assistant entered the room. My attorney, Lisa Schrieversdorf, walked over to them and tried to negotiate a better deal. By the way they were talking, it wasn't looking good and I began to cry.

Everyone in the courtroom stood up, when the judge entered the room. The only sound you heard was the judge as he walked to the bench and sat down. He then called the prosecutor and my attorney to the bench. The only sound I heard then was the pounding in my chest. What only took a few minutes seemed like hours. The mood between the judge, the prosecutor and Lisa was very serious, with constant issues exchanged back and forth. Finally, they all stopped talking and the muscles on their faces relaxed into smiles and Lisa and the prosecutor shook hands. Lisa turned and gave me a smile. She presented me with a document that had to be signed by me, the prosecution and the judge.

Jesus must have heard my prayers for the second time. Thank you, Jesus. My attorney negotiated the plea bargain to the three months of time served at Riker's Island, and five years' probation.

Following is that document.

January 25, 1995

The Sentencing Document

SUPREME COURT OF THE STATE OF NEW YORK
ADVISEMENT TO DEFENDANT

FAILURE TO CONFORM TO ANY OF THE FOLLOWING CONDITIONS OF YOUR PROBATION, INCLUDING THE FAILURE TO REPORT TO YOUR PROBATION OFFICER, IS A VIOLATION OF PROBATION.

YOU HAVE A RIGHT TO BE PRESENT AT ANY HEARING TO DETERMINE WHETHER A VIOLATION OF PROBATION HAS OCCURRED. IF YOU INTENTIONALLY ABSENT YOURSELF FROM THE COURT'S JURISDICTION OR INTENTIONALLY FAIL TO APPEAR AT A VIOLATION OF PROBATION HEARING, A HEARING MAY BE HELD IN YOUR ABSENCE, AND A REVOCATION OF YOUR PROBATION MAY RESULT.

SUPREME COURT OF N.Y. STATE

COUNTY OF KINGS

PEOPLE OF THE STATE OF NEW YORK,
—against—

GLORIA DeLAURENTIS

Ind./Docket No. 3098-94

CONDITIONS OF PROBATION

Defendant

THE ABOVE NAMED DEFENDANT HAVING BEEN
convicted of the crime of Manslaughter 2°

found to be a youthful offender for the criminal act of

or the criminal action entitled above

and having been sentenced to

a _____ term of imprisonment, and to

a 5 year period of probation to expire on _____ unless terminated sooner in accordance with the Criminal Procedure Law

and to pay a fine in the amount of $_____

P.S.

ORDERED, that during the period of probation the defendant shall comply with the following conditions and any other conditions which the Court may impose at any time prior to the expiration of the period of probation.

PROBATION CONDITIONS:—THE PROBATIONER SHALL:

1. Report to a probation officer as directed by the Court or the probation officer and permit the probation officer to visit his or her place of abode or elsewhere.

   (A) Report immediately to 210 Joralemon Street, Brooklyn, NY 11201

   B) Upon release from custody report immediately to _____

2. Remain within the jurisdiction of the Court unless granted permission to leave by the Court or the probation officer.

3. Answer all reasonable inquiries by the probation officer and notify the probation officer prior to any change in address or employment.
   Pay such restitution or reparation, together with a designated surcharge of $_____ to _____

   Name of Restitution Agency

13. Perform services for a public or not-for-profit corporation, association, institution or agency, as follows: _____

14. Spend a specified part of this sentence at a division for youth facility or attend a nonresidential program pursuant to P.L. §65.10(2)(d), as follows: _____

15. Post a bond or security in the amount of $_____ for the performance of any or all conditions imposed.

16. Observe the specified conditions or conduct as set forth in an order or prohibition issued pursuant to CPL §530.12.

17. Comply with the following conditions which the court deems to be reasonably related to his or her rehabilitation: _____

18. Obey the directions given by the probation officer to insure compliance with the Conditions of Probation.

Dated: Brooklyn, New York
JAN 25 19 95

ENTER

Hon. Lewis Douglass J.S.O.

Agency/Judge

RECEIPT

I have this day received a copy of the foregoing Conditions of Probation.

Dated: 1/25/95

Witness (Court Clerk)

(Signature)

Gloria DeLaurentis

Defendant

(Signature)

COURT COPY - ATTACH TO CASE RECORD

The Truth Set Me Free

At one point, when I went to visit my kids, Patrick's father was there. He asked to speak to me alone. I hesitated at first, but I knew it wasn't my time to die. Tomorrow was another day. I stood before him and for a moment he just stared at me, before saying, "I'm going to kill you, not now, but soon."

I looked at him. I hadn't planned to say what I did, it just came out. "I didn't kill your son, I put him at rest. He was a tortured soul. He's home with Jesus now."

Patrick used to tell me how his mother abused him, starting at age seven or eight. His two sisters also sexually abused him. They played with his penis and kissed him all over. That's what he told me, but that's no reason for him to take it out on me and subject my kids to his sickness. When I told my sister what I told his father, she said, "If he was

with Jesus, I'm sure he isn't living in the main house
or around any of God's other children."

The End

After sentencing, I wasn't truly free. I'm presently in a mandatory forensic program at the Sun Coast Mental Health Clinic, where anyone who ever killed anyone becomes a permanent member. I suffer from PTSD Syndrome and they provide psychiatric and financial aid. I'm still working to prove that I've changed. I want to see my kids, but their lives are busy and whatever. Even with the plea bargain I will be in the program for life which further prevents me from putting this tragedy behind me.

My kids, after I killed Patrick initially went to my sister-in-law's home and later went into foster care. Patrick Jr. is now 31, David—26, and Dominic—25. None of my children want anything to do with me. They say they're afraid of me. I've been told that my son David, was so traumatized that he would never date a white woman. He thinks they are all crazy. Do you believe that? David now has a black wife and child. There are all these lies going around that my kids had a sad life. My son Patrick, on his eighteenth birthday said that when he was nine, I gave him crack. And my son Dominic, lived with two gay men because he was scared of women. Do you believe that's even possible?

I hope my story will provide some money to help my kids and grandchildren. And maybe help women who are being abused get out of their situations before it's too late.